WISH
LESS
WORK
more

WORK
HARD
STAY
STRONG

Every
Moment
Is A Fresh
Beginning

BE THE
Best
VERSION
of you

STRIVE
FOR
PROGRESS
NOT
PERFECTION

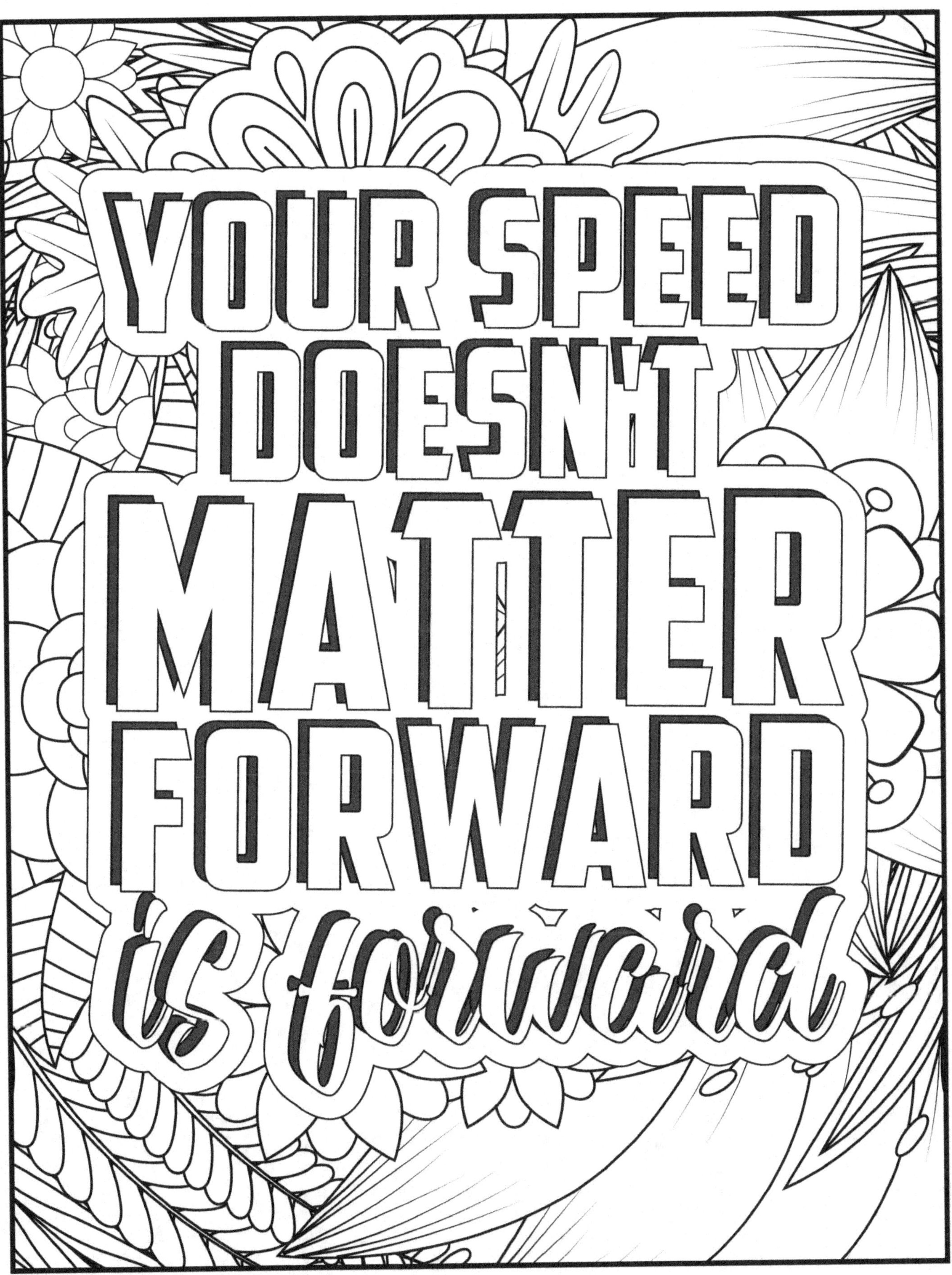

YOUR SPEED
DOESN'T
MATTER
FORWARD
is forward

DREAM
WITHOUT
fear

life is
TOUGH
BUT SO
ARE YOU

TURN
i wish
INTO
i will

EVERYDAY
is a
FRESH
start

I Am Working
ON MYSELF
FOR MYSELF
BY MYSELF

THE BEST
is yet
TO
COME

today
ANYTHING
is
POSSIBLE

ONE DAY
OR
DAY ONE
YOU DECIDE

STRIVE
FOR
PROGRESS
NOT
PERFECTION

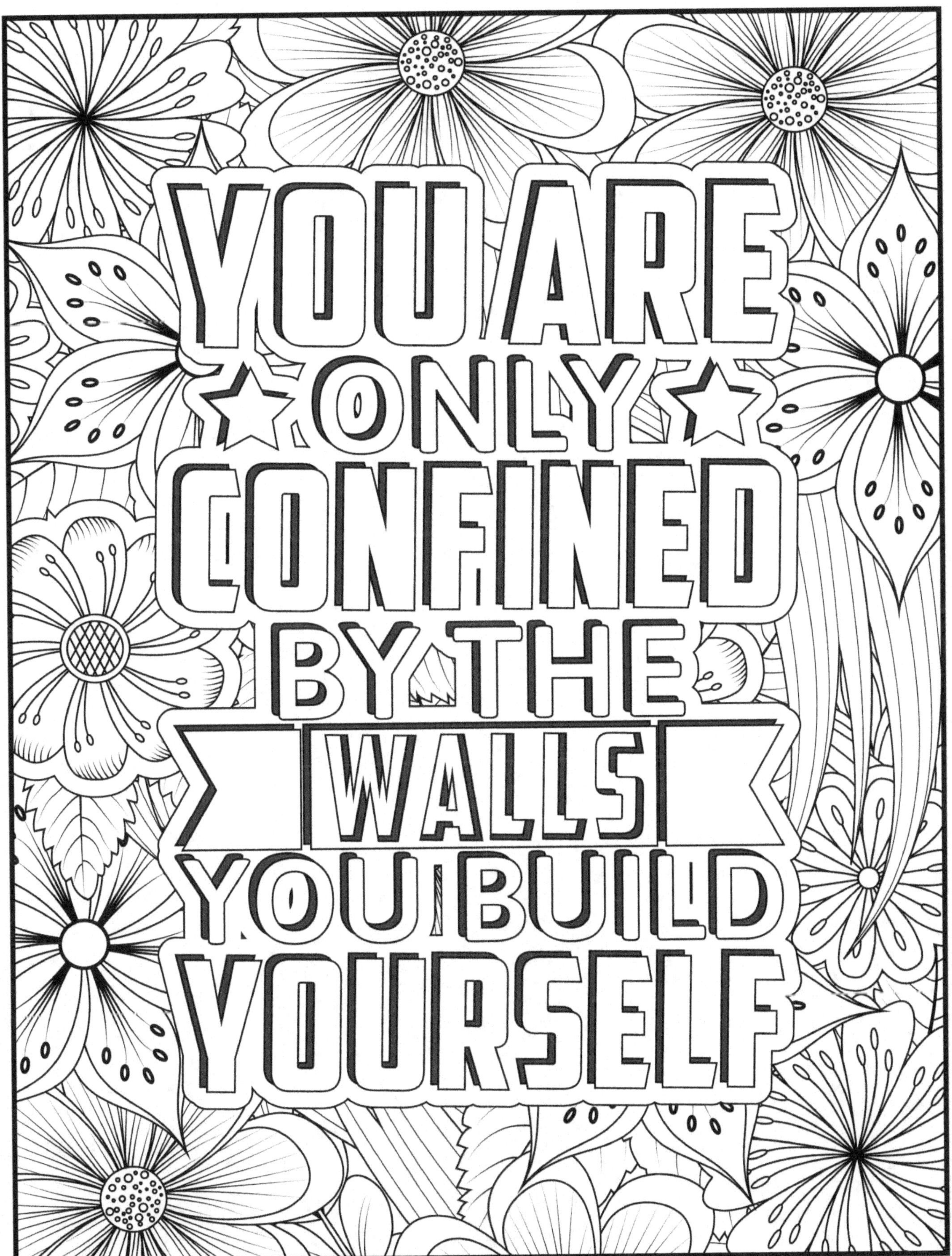

YOU ARE
ONLY
CONFINED
BY THE
WALLS
YOU BUILD
YOURSELF

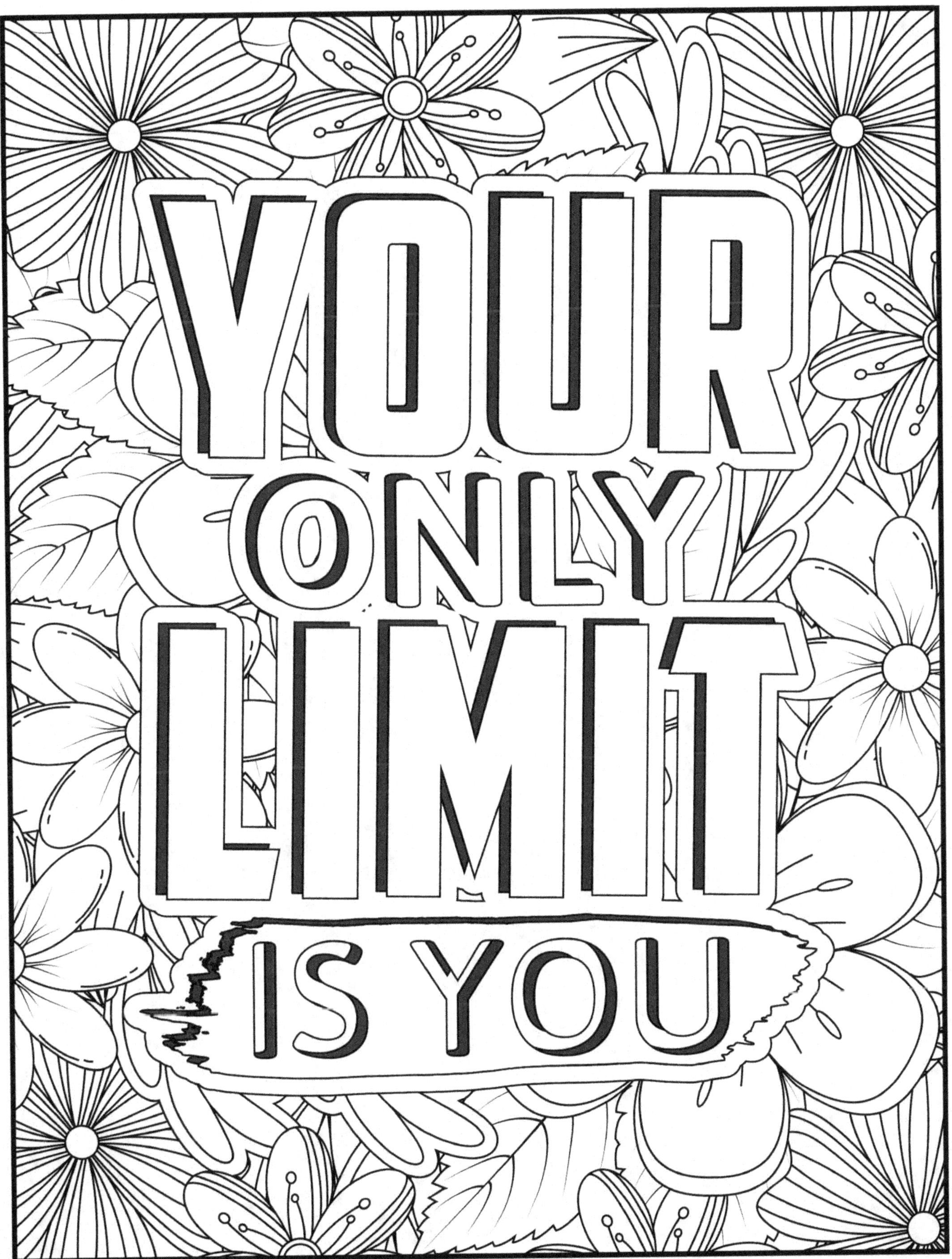
YOUR
ONLY
LIMIT
IS YOU

Don't
STOP
UNTIL
YOU'RE
PROUD

KEEP
GOING
KEEP
GROWING

MAKE
TODAY
RIDICULOUSLY
AMAZING

NOTHING
EASY IS
WORTH
DOING

AIM
HIGHER
DREAM
BIGGER

LET YOUR
dreams
BE YOUR
WINGS

YOU ARE NEVER
Too Old
TO LEARN

Nothing
EASY IS
WORTH
DOING

GET OUT
OF
YOUR
own way

GRACE
and
HUSTLE

Follow
your
Dreams
they know the
way

FALLING DOWN
IS AN
ACCIDENT!
staying down
is a
CHOICE

Don't stop
until you
are
proud

DO LESS
with
MORE
FOCUS

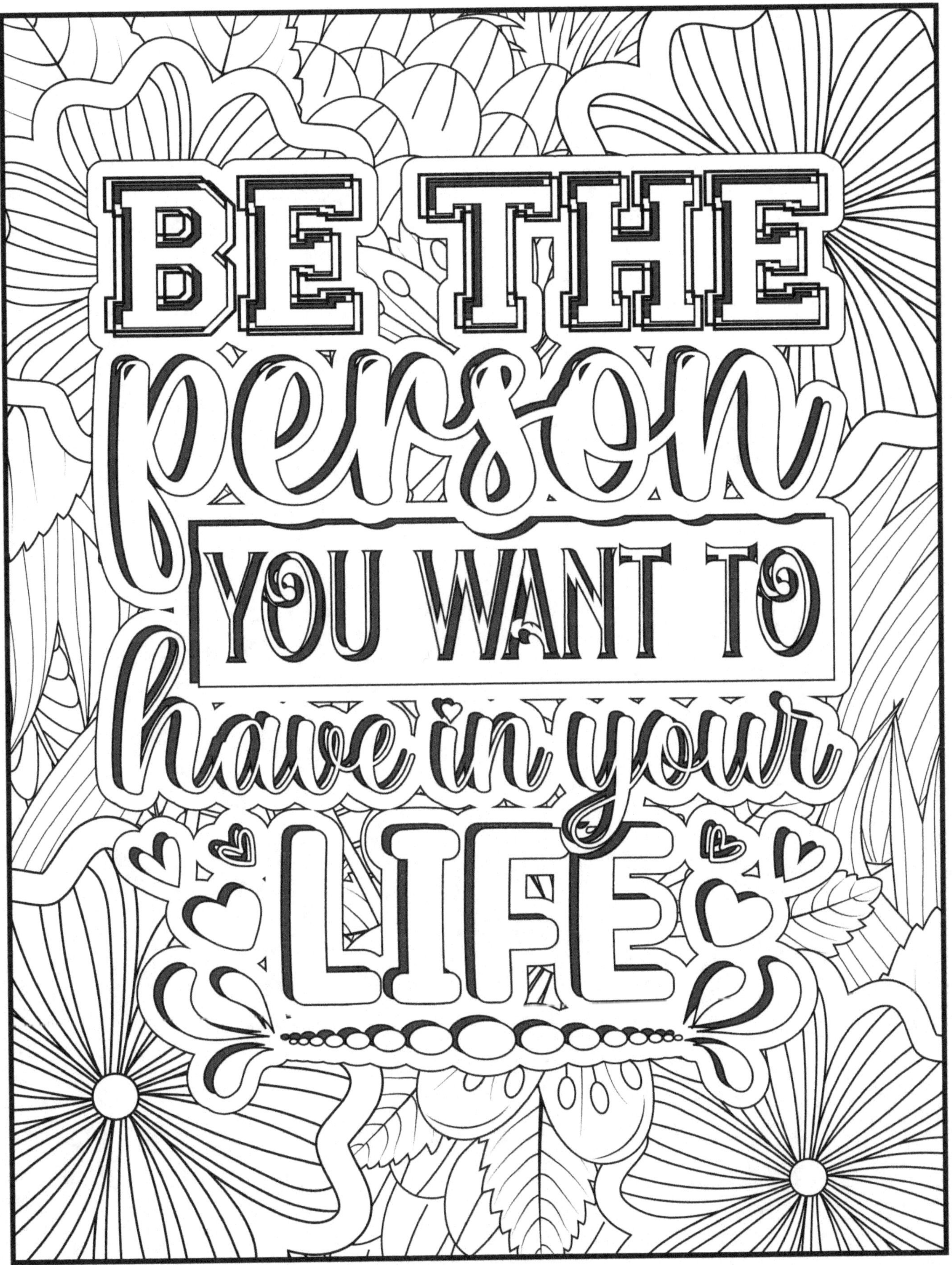

BE THE
person
YOU WANT TO
have in your
LIFE

Do ALL
Things
WITH
LOVE

inhale
the future
exhale
the past

ALWAYS
BE
KIND

Be
KIND

NEVER
Stop
Looking Up

DREAM
WISH IT
IT DO IT

DON'T
CALL IT A
DREAM
CALL IT A
PLAN

STRiVE
for
PROGRESS
not
PERFECTION

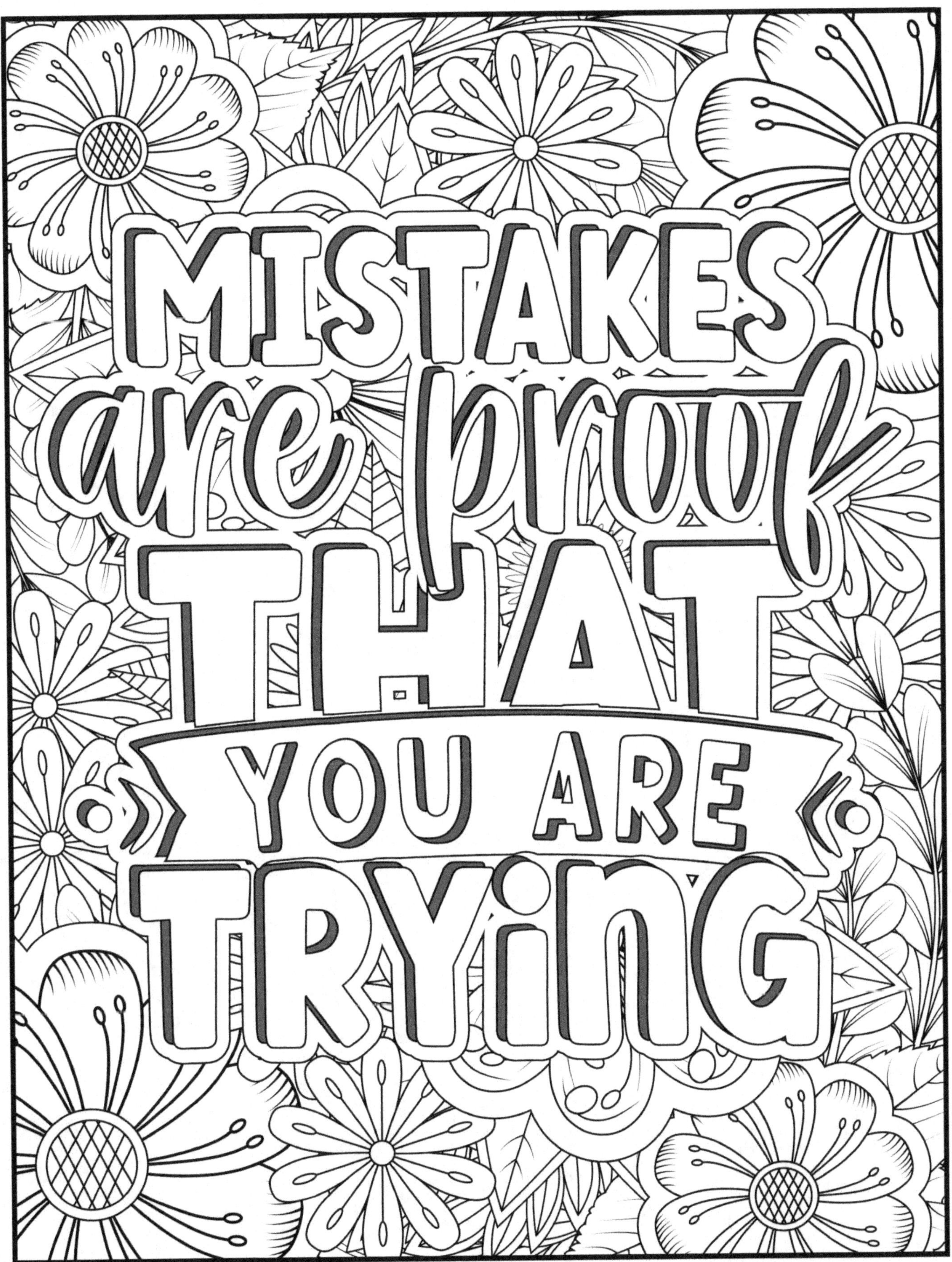

MISTAKES
are proof
THAT
YOU ARE
TRYING

I AM
Working
ON MYSELF
FOR MY SELF
BY MY SELF

WiSH
less work
MORE

GOOD
Things
TAKE
TIME

BE THE
Nice
KID

YOU ARE
Living
YOUR
STORY

TURN
I WISH
INTO
I WILL

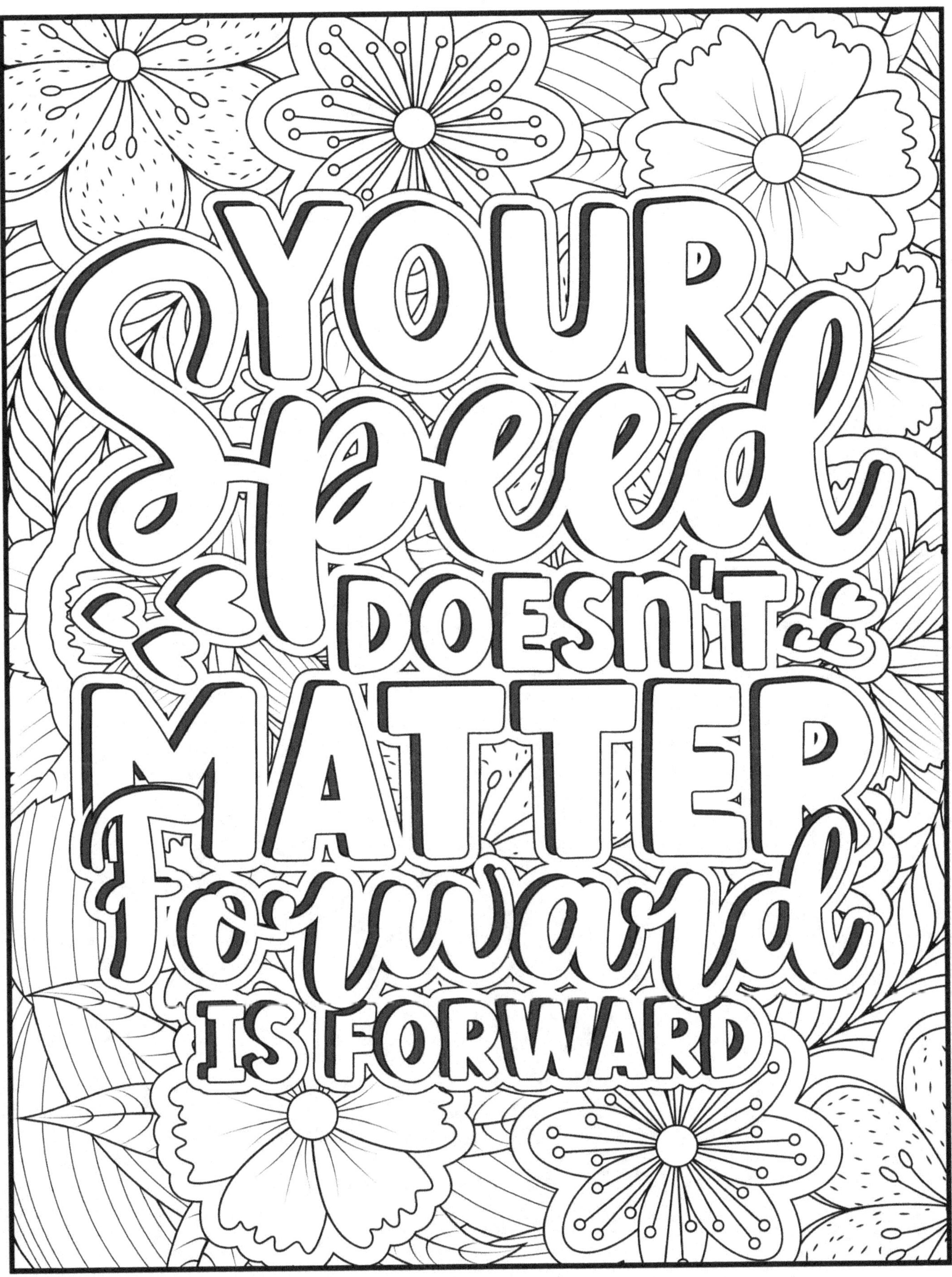

YOUR
SPEED
DOESN'T
MATTER
Forward
IS FORWARD

DREAM
Without
FEAR

YOU ARE
never too
OLD TO
Learn